This Strong Mercy

First Warbler Press Edition 2025

This Strong Mercy: Poems of Collapse and Reimagining
© 2025 Linda C. Welsh

warblerpress.com

ISBN 978-1-965684-76-4 (hardcover)
ISBN 978-1-965684-75-7 (paperback)
ISBN 978-1-965684-77-1 (e-book)

This Strong Mercy

Poems of Collapse
and Reimagining

LINDA C. WELSH

warbler press

CONTENTS

This Strong Mercy. 1

A Perfection 3

AMOC 5

Incantations 10

Apple Tree. 11

Compass 13

Biosphere 15

Fibonacci of Survival. 18

All At Once 21

West Antarctic Ice Sheet 24

Flying Blind 26

Turning Toward Tomorrow 28

Attend 29

Tipping Point 31

I Lived 33

A War Against Ourselves 35

Simple and Hollow 38

Circular Pattern. 40

Warm Water Coral Reefs 42

Atoll 46

The Holocene 48

Polyculture 50

Musings. 51

Table Runner Couture 52

A New Blueness 54

Permafrost 56

Threshold 58

Ashes and Seedlings 60

Potential 62

A Soft Place to Fall. 65

CONTENTS

Stillness 68
Adaptation Plan. 69
Thwaites Glacier 72
The Ground of Being 74
Gleanings 77
Full On. 78
Oppression 79
Mutualistic Power 81
Immunity 82
Earthward 83
Lungs 85
Cascade 87
Hush, Little Baby. 89
Erosional Remnant 91
The Voices of Change 94
Ceaseless Vibration. 97
Light that Persists Unseen. 99
Shadow Song 101
Papery Divinity 104
Deer Botany 106
The Weight of Ice 109
Unburdened Heart 111
Embers and Wind 113
Calm. 115
Listen 117
Call and Response. 120
Prairie Smoke. 123
All the Darknesses We Have Lived 124

*"My desires are many and my cry is pitiful,
but ever didst thou save me by hard refusals;
and this strong mercy has been wrought into
my life through and through."*
—Rabindranath Tagore

This Strong Mercy

For Susan

She was out of options she could love—
the only thing left: this strong mercy
in the bullet of her gun.

Eighty years old when she drove
down the Ruby River Valley
toward the beloved home
that was no longer hers.
Bumped down the gravel washboard
road in the rented car.
Took in the view of the white
piercing mountain peaks.
Tipped her head back and
pulled the trigger.

She was an expression of earth's beauty,
intelligence and design. She was not
plagued by weak, uncertain desire—yet
patterns have an insidious pull
like the capsized canoe
pressed against the brambles
by the river's current.

Surrendering to gravity's insistent sway
we hold the bind of knowing too much,
and doing too little, our maps unwittingly written
into body and mind, paths to
consequences we do not intend.

After the finality of extinction
comes reflection and a seeking plea.
Upheld on stilts of guilt and grief, mortality
and motivation groan in the commons
we all share.

In this labyrinth of living
our choices can lead to
points of no return;
game over, but no end in sight just
the wail of an old throat
in the pristine valley.

A Perfection

In-breath, out-breath in the dark,
the fridge humming
its optimistic tune.
This infinite moment,
in the blue light glow
of the digital screen-in-bloom.

The stiff silence upholds
the omnipresent question—
its bent pages a sign of passersby
who rushed to find answers
in the blustery stories of mind.

And down the stairs from the second floor,
the footfalls of history impress—
stories I'd rather not make a part of myself—
but that explain inborn fears
and in-worn tears not from this present life,
but resounding from the deepest past,
like the three-toed prints of the Eubrontes dinosaur,
captured in sandstone for 200 million years.

Are there not encoded texts everywhere?

Last night in the garden,
two Great Grey Owls surfed the silver glow of air—
like the mobile over the crib.
Their distinctive facial disks funneling sound
to their offset ears, hunting with hearing alone.

The nautilus shell pendant hanging from my neck—

her precise spiral symmetry,
the golden ratio—harmony, elegance.

The hexagonal cells of the honeycomb—
with their sweet, warm scent of hay, leather and musk,
a balance of function and form,
maximizing space with minimal material—
a marvel of sacred geometry
burning now in the form of a candle
shaped like a lotus flower.

These myriad wonders permeate every scale—
life imbued with Spirit, inspiration, and intelligence:
patterns and principles to measure living by.

Good and ill, right and wrong—
the dichotomies of cultures:
the jagged edges of apprehension,
the debates and struggles for equity;
dualities' particular weight—
the ignorance, the suffering, the hate.

Timeless, demonstrable truths
etched in the living world's flesh,
ripple in the pulse of rivers and roots,
palpable perfection, unseen yet knowable.

Outside, after the rare rain,
a single dew-laden web catches the sun—
its delicate threads glinting like silver veins;
while the robins, newly here, flash their rusty chests
on the periphery of my visual field.

AMOC

The phrase "Atlantic Meridional Overturning
    Circulation"
is like a too big bite of burrito,
cabbage falling out of the corners
of my mouth.
What is it, and why
is it insinuating itself into my
consciousness?

"Atlantic" refers to the Atlantic Ocean,
second to the Pacific Ocean in size,
but a part of the grand and interconnected
global ocean of planet Earth.

"Meridional" refers to a north-south orientation:
Movement toward the north pole
is northerly in direction;
movement toward the south pole
is southerly in direction.
A north-south orientation,
like longitudinal lines,
like the granite mountain ridge,
the migration of birds,
your spine and mine.

"Overturning" refers to the
different layers of ocean water
rising and sinking relative to each other,
depending on their
temperature and salinity.

This process has a three-dimensional
component where the water
on the surface of the ocean
can sink to the deep reaches of the sea.
The deep reaches,
where squid, krill, jellies and fish
live in the dark.

"Circulation" refers to flow.
This current shifts more water
every second
than every river in the world
combined!
Flow, like our blood; like
our lymph; like
our speech; like
our love-making; like
the child putting everything
in her mouth—
seeing, feeling, tasting, touching,
experiencing the mysterious world.

The AMOC: our world's enormous
conveyor belt whisk, which provides
essential ingredients necessary for life
and distributes heat energy around
our planet, is weakening.

GESTURE

The sea, once teeming
with glorious and mysterious life,
is the single most powerful sculptor
of our planet and our lives.

Sea water flows across
the Atlantic towards Europe.

As it flows, some of its heat is lost
to the atmosphere through evaporation,
making temperatures in Europe about
10°C warmer than areas
in the same latitude in the U.S.
Imagine palm trees in Sweden - yes.
Would there be palm trees in southern
Alaska? No.

This evaporation only takes water
and not the salt.
So the concentration of salt in the
remaining water increases along the way.

Listen, eventually the warm salty water hits
the cold fresh water below the arctic circle,
an invitation to tango!
And because the salty water is denser,
it sinks and gets caught up in the deep
southerly currents that carry it all the way
south, around Antarctica, across the Indian
and Pacific Oceans, eventually back up
to join the Gulf Stream once more.

The whole circuit can take up to
1,000 years to complete.

A SLAP OF AHA!

In what high esteem we must hold
this temperate veil!

Assume the worshipful posture of the
Mediterranean fennel with its chunky stems—
the ones waved by ecstatic followers
of the Greek god Dionysus!
This plant's life made possible by the AMOC,
which brings warm tropical water
to her sweetly aromatic leaves
in Europe!

We need a functioning AMOC to ensure
livable weather for all life on this
planet.

METAMORPHOSIS

Climate change is affecting
this global circulation system.
The melting of ice from the arctic ocean
and from the Greenland ice sheet vastly
increases the amount of fresh water
in the surrounding seas.
As the water freshens and becomes less salty
the sea water gets less dense and less likely
to sink and join up with the deep cold currents.
This slows down the AMOC system.

The AMOC is the weakest it has been
in 1600 years.

HUMILITY

The slowdown or shutdown of the AMOC
in this century is possible.
Abrupt changes, stretching
around the globe

will affect all the life support
systems on the planet.

Their worried faces blaze,
from far away.
It's as though I am absent;
their warnings do not touch me.
I acknowledge the threat yet
simultaneously deny it—
in this perverse state
of mind.

SUPPLICATION

You are visible and responsive.
You are powerful, persistently
like an accelerating airplane
taking off.

You are the Giver.
Do not be taciturn
and indifferent like an old
roll of stamps.
You are capable of turning
the course of our lives onto
paths of regeneration and not
of degradation. Consciousness now
awakened, this power, oh life!
Will you allow it to send us back
to the beginning,
again?

Incantations

I have not heard your voice,
nor have I listened in stillness lately.
But I have seen your movements
in wind-blown trees, in the warbler songs:
incantations on the chirping patio.

I have seen your face
in the faces of those around me.
And I have noticed your spirit whispering—
all through the day and night—
your footprints on the snowy path to my door.

When the light is short,
and the weight of my body
is tethered to the stake of remembrance,
I feel you.
Yours is the power of the seed—
size of a pinhead—
becoming the largest being on this planet: Sequoia.

No one has enough information to be pessimistic.
After all, your wild edges birth galaxies.

Apple Tree

An upturned palm with rounded fingers, the Kerr
Crabapple Tree. She is the most willing apple in my
high-elevation garden, with fruit offerings every year.
Her cherry-red orbs, the size of golf balls, press into
red punch that packs a puckering mouthful of sweet
and astringent flavors. Her style and her scent speak
of all the seasons she has lived. Her body's red-tinged
flesh becomes a part of me in this festival of invisible
chemistry.

The ripening of apples on my valiant tree is governed
by a positive feedback loop driven by a gas called
ethylene. As the first apple matures, it releases this
plant hormone that accelerates ripening. Nearby
apples sense this signal and begin producing their
own ethylene, magnifying the miracle. This chain
reaction creates a wave of ripening across the tree.

This chemical dance mirrors larger patterns in nature—
how small shifts ripple outward to shape entire
ecosystems. The rapid transition from unripe to
overripe fruit reveals how one change can cascade,
amplifying further changes *in the same direction.*

I wonder at the power of a single act of kindness, for
example—one wise act, one visionary moment. I
imagine a wild conflagration of caring spreading in
countless iterations across the vast tree of life that
is everything we have ever known and everything
we have ever loved. Tangled up together as we are,
we can sway the surge toward renewal or toward

degradation and the song of collapse.

Our passing—and pass we shall—may it be as gentle as a little ripe apple releasing itself from the branch: falling sweetly to the yielding earth, luminous with possibility, merging into its next form within creation's vast design.

Compass

A finger of fear
tightens around my throat
when I read the daily news.
My world feels disoriented:
my clothes, my shoes,
the tan-tongued toothbrush—
all wonder about coping.

Do I have needed resources—
what about those who don't?
Confusion about what
the data means, deepens—
these lost hours without a map.

I see myself in fevered dreams,
slick with regret in the dark—
anxiety up close.
Like the feeling of wading too far
into the sea and losing, suddenly,
contact with the ground.

Yet in the morning,
the comfrey's hairy leaves,
and her jangling amethyst flowers,
ring with joy.
Life leans toward life;
we are part of the gift.
I set my course into this leaning.

Beloved friend, we have not lost our compass.
You show me the flowering structures:

the pistil and stamen,
my body, yours,
and the cloudless sky.
The little green hummingbird
sips of the columbine flowers
and agrees.

And beneath our towering
mountain ranges,
with their power and silent snows—
the Valerian stands up so sturdily,
so confidently, on her green steed!

The beckoning winds
ply our doors—
a stunning, powerful sound—
while the neighbor keeps pigs,
whose odors waft in.

Biosphere

Living skin of Earth,
Guide me to where the crystalline river of sound reason
flows freely, undammed by affluence,
unbroken in its course,
spreading in ever-widening ripples of inclusion—
nourishing even future generations—
into that heaven of sanity
we may peacefully die into.

Home of all life—
in the air, on land and beneath the sea—
you birth us, cradle us, and sustain us.
We are part of you, Beloved.
Mother, Father, Creator: Biosphere.

My mother taught me duty; my father taught me care—
planting fruit trees and gardens against the ghost
   of scarcity.
Yet neither spoke your name,
though I found you in yellow grassy fields and gnarly
   oak trees,
friends I knew at once how to love.
I do not recall learning anything more about you—
not at home, not at school.

What was the power that cracked curiosity open—
like a brown egg split at the edge of cast iron;
yolk spreading golden across the hot pan?
It was your splendor—your breath-taking intricacies,
and mind-blowing panoramas.
It was the life teeming in your soil, air, water and light

that spoke intimately to my soul.

Living sky of Earth,
Our values and habits undermine your ability to sustain
    us.
We consume more than your capacity to provide,
and spew out more waste than you can bear to absorb.
Is the climatic chaos we now face merely
a stark reflection of your truth—
a truth maturing in all your fearsome fury?

Lay my wounded body upon the forest floor.
Fold my shallowness into the musty pine duff, tucked in.
Let me feel the sweet web of you.

Living water of Earth,
Our vision is short-sighted; our systems built to match.
Week after week, we unknowingly consume
the equivalent of a credit card's worth
of plastic—through our food, water, and air. Oh Beloved,
our waste has entered into the very fabric of life.
This wondrous layer of existence clings to your rounded
    embrace;
yet our trash has become both your body and ours.

Living Biosphere,
The babe cries—its wail sounding hunger and longing.
Gushing in response, the mother's full breast
    pours out her nourishment—
immediately, abundantly, without hesitation or
    restraint.

How I love you.
I will fight for you—not alone, but with all

who hear your cry and refuse to turn away.
Together we will mend what we have broken,
restore what we have taken,
and learn again to live as part of your living skin.

Fibonacci of Survival

I.

We camped on a desert bluff—
looked out upon a vast canvas
of eroded, callused ridges.
Up close, cactus bloomed—
yellow, red, orange and white—
symmetrical spines arranged
in the sacred Fibonacci spiral.
This miracle,
a vision of hope.

Plants grew like a tended garden—
silent spaces in-between mirrored
our singular awe.
Life here persists and adapts
in sweltering days and freezing nights.

Deeply tranquil but for the desiccating wind,
we were infinitesimal beneath the boisterously
performing symphony of night sky.

By morning, I had aged 100 years—
wrinkles I had never loved before
were like the creased landscape,
where time layers and collapses.

The over-grazed, dead soil waits—
a patient opportunity for microbes
to make life possible again.
I, too, carry this quiet hope,

that life can re-imagine itself in me.

The perennial cooing of a dove—
syrinx vibrating in her chest—
followed me from place to place:
a purring kind of music that crooned of survival—
of landscapes transforming.

2.

One third of the Earth's land is now desert.
Some deserts are spreading their strong wings,
claiming more ground as their own—
while plant life recedes.

I wondered: How might people survive here?
Eat the seeds of creosote, like the desert packrat?
No threat of starvation then.

3.

The mountains lay seductive in their tan threads
trimmed with splashes of white, rust and jade jewels.
Thirst as absolute as an island's.

The mesquite tree, with roots reaching down fifty feet
    to water—
theirs is a kind of certainty in this washed-out land—
that threatens water everywhere with "flood zone"
    warnings,
yet holds onto none of it.

It is roasting—this arid, breathless place,

clinging persistently to new interpretations of life.

The buzz of flies hover in the air—
in this landscape of perpetual becoming,
where we are all migrants—skin sleek with sweat,
breath borrowed from wind.

We map survival,
not in straight lines, but in spirals:
each act a negotiation and a listening,
each moment a seed waiting to crack open
beneath an indifferent sky.

All At Once

All at once
summer comes to my bed—
a golden gown of light laid
across my pillow,
her warmth whispering.

Here, in this tiny shaft of light,
hope stretches and yawns.
The pettiness of thought,
a persistent hum,
while parsley and sage toss
and roil in their verdant beds
of cool, moist soil.

l knead the earth,
pull the purslane—
the color of your eyes.
In you groans my
last chance to forge
a deeper nature connection.

The thirsty cottonwood trees
remember the fullness of sap rising,
while hope for a generous,
water-bearing sky
and full harvest baskets
ripen.

Then, all at once,
autumn undresses in the brisk
air, whispering release.

I smooth the red and yellow
flowery tablecloth, set a vase
of Angel Wing Begonia cuttings
on the Lazy Susan.
Salt, pepper, and a smokey quartz crystal
beckon: "Come for tea,
oh seasons that flash
so suddenly in this wildness.
Tell me about your worries,
and I will tell you mine."

Mid-sentence—and all at once—
winter comes to my lengthening shadow,
reaching her fingers
through doors shut tight,
entering regal and entitled.

Don't you know the saying
about a guest that stays
too long?

Your insistent rolfing changes our shape;
our bodies surrender
to the relief of being powerless.

And all at once, the soft,
flowing hair of the mountain
tickles the window ledge,
announcing spring.
Rambling vines and hibiscus scent fill
the hollow spaces of my heart.

The festering cold dissolves
into emerging green.

Lucky forests swell
with moisture and scent—
like your arousal.

I was alone in my life
like an empty school yard when—
all at once—
Canada geese streaked the sky
like tubas of hello!

Your paddle and mine stroking
the body of the river—
I watch my defeats now
from a long way off.

West Antarctic Ice Sheet

The lush, warm rainforest thrived in balmy 66°F (19°C) days, showcasing a palette of a thousand shades of green—malachite, lime, aquamarine, mint, pine—and hues with yellow, gray, and blue undertones adding depth and texture to the scene. The dense web of vegetation pulsed with life. Ancient seedless vascular plants waved their feather-like fronds in the low-angle sunlight. Conifer trees and flowering plants, similar to those found in Australia and New Zealand, filled every ecological niche. Antarctica was a verdant garden, where dinosaurs roamed in a tropical paradise. However, tectonic shifts and climatic changes gradually transformed this once-hospitable continent into the most uninhabitable place on Earth.

Today, this immense continent—1.5 times the size of the United States—is Earth's largest desert and coldest region, holding a record low temperature of -128.6°F (-89.2°C), recorded at Vostok Station in 1983. Beneath its miles-thick ice cap lies a hidden world of over 400 subglacial lakes, while its shimmering surface holds 90% of Earth's ice. Antarctica is a shape-shifting land of extremes: the coldest, windiest, driest, and highest continent on Earth, with an average elevation of 8,200 feet.

The West Antarctic Ice Sheet (WAIS), a vast expanse of ice resting on bedrock below sea level, is experiencing accelerated melting due to warming ocean waters in the Amundsen Sea. This process is driven by marine ice sheet instability, where warmer waters erode ice shelves that act as barriers to inland glaciers. Studies suggest that this melting is now largely unavoidable—even under ambitious climate targets—as ocean temperatures are projected to rise at nearly three times their historical rate this century.

The collapse of WAIS could unleash an estimated 5.3-meter (17.4-foot) rise in global sea levels—enough to reshape coastlines and submerge major cities like New York, Tokyo, and London. This catastrophic change would displace hundreds of millions of people and disrupt ecosystems worldwide.

This fragile, vast, and frigid ecosystem waits for its cue—rehearsing now for a dramatic entrance onto the world stage. Will her brilliant ark open, unveiling a new form as global warming extends its invitation to awaken? Where we see instability, WAIS embodies transformation—solidity dissolving into seas that will reshape our world.

Flying Blind

From the darkness,
flying blind into the vast threat,
I surrender
into your sweetness.

Pine needles up close look
like striped zucchini!
I never knew.

The tiny hairs on the mosses—
whole forested worlds,
including giants and fairies.
Plants, going about the business
of fixing carbon dioxide
and releasing oxygen,
I never knew.

The microscopic world
on my skin—bizarre.
I have been made so permeable,
part of Earth's physiology.
I never knew.

2.

The spotted fawn lay
dying on the road.
His blue lungs and heart,
electrified for beating—

his parts the same as mine.
His eyes, grey and glossy...
l believe his spirit has taken flight.
Run, beloved, through the
thorny thicket—
free.

3.

The snowflakes today—so large,
the sky's nostrils flared,
blowing out the icy contagion.

While the magpies perch,
then dive—
their splayed-out wings
fanning the infected air.

Turning Toward Tomorrow

With my light backpack,
easy behind me,
I hike over grassy hills in Navarra—their slopes
dotted with twirling white wind turbines—
stirring hope, welcoming in:
an age free of fossil fuels.

The air smells of coming rain
in the energetic waves of wind.
I imagine every step I take
healing, not harming.

Attend

The Osprey swoops out of the sapphire sky
like glass shards of surprise,
to pluck the fish
from the singing river.
One truth I know—

The insane coupling
of progress and might,
without self-interest,
by which we foul
the very air, soil, and water
on which our lives depend.
This ignorance I know—

My old clingy suffering,
like the ivy on the bedroom ceiling,
incanting,
"You were wrong."
This regret I know—

Cirrus clouds:
hairy filaments of silk,
icy sheen, colored by a palette
of bright yellow and red lit up—
drawn-out whispers fading to gray.
This awe I know—

Our truths take flight
on the melodies from every tooth,
harmonies from every hair,
all breaking forth in the flower song

of skin, nails and the instrument
of our fluted driftwood bones!

Oh world of infinite wonders—
sea, earth and sky taken together
speak about the whole:
The Way, the reason for laughter,
the pull of remembrance—
the tragedy—
of forgetting.

Tipping Point

I believe some of us will succeed
in re-imagining the way we live
on this earth.
We will have to endure
many things.
But if we align with the living world
and her 3.8 billion years of problem-solving know-how,
we will overcome every challenge we face.

Consider frogs, for example—
Wood frogs can freeze solid in winter
and then come back to life when they thaw.
Their body produces a special "antifreeze" sugar
that protects their cells, allowing them to survive
        temperatures
far below freezing.
When spring comes, they simply defrost
and hop away like nothing happened.
It's like nature's own pause button—
for a frog.

Life adapts in astonishing ways:
tardigrades—microscopic organisms—
can survive extreme heat (above 300°F),
intense cold (near absolute zero), radiation,
and even the vacuum of space
by entering a cryptobiotic state!
Pompeii worms, found near hydrothermal vents,
thrive in water temperatures up to 176°F
and rely on symbiotic bacteria for survival.
From cell to cosmos, adaptation weaves

a patient, unrelenting narrative.

To survive, I trust in the power that is LIFE—
even if, one day, only cockroaches,
dromedary camels, and resilient bacteria are all that
    remain
to fill the pages of life's encyclopedia of wonders.
While tardigrades drift through the vacuum of space,
life's intelligent doggedness, will assert itself—
spanning every field, every niche,
and into the days called tomorrow.

Beloved, supreme ignorances of all kinds
have always enacted their sinister crimes
on game-board Earth and her peoples.
Some days, I fear that no one is watching.
But today, my life is dressed in geranium leggings
and a green velvet dress—
for life does not merely survive;
it incants, it roars, it transforms—an unstoppable
    symphony
of innovation that echoes from the first trembling cell
to the complex consciousness of today.

I believe in the process that is LIFE—
even if, for a time, there is just trouble.

I Lived

I lived
where you can hear
the wing flaps of raven
and the rotor blades
of the wind generator whoosh—
in full bloom, year-around.

I lived
where the bobcat slipped
through the checkerboard of fir trees,
with the openness of a hoo-hoo owl
in the evening light.
Where the smell of pine and sage
was thick as honey.

I lived
in fear and incredulity
as the most pessimistic climate models
turned out to be understatements.

I lived
with a sad story to understand
what was happening in my country.

I lived
far from political spectacles and debates—
just orange coals in the chittering fire,
and the glowing, alarming news.

I lived
with anger: Those with true power,

sheltered from the worst
of climate instability, deny it.

I lived
with sadness: grief that our hunger and greed
created a vast emptiness in wilderness;
rage for the silences and contamination
I found there.

I lived
where the rain stopped—like my stepfather,
who died of melanoma two days before Christmas.
Prayers, his last words for days.

I lived
to quell the waves
of my mother's dementia.
Her name: Solitude—like the distances between us,
my steps forward coming from bare ground.

I lived
where no mountain hid the sun,
or earth's child—the moon.
Where the fullness of my days ripened
like a plum.

I lived
in hope—hope and trust in the preeminence
of the living world: her sediments miles deep,
her sea mountains taller than those on land.

Our beautiful boat, now beached
on the predicament of our world,
is where I am now.

A War Against Ourselves

In the smoky haze that drifts low in the valley,
my apprehensions float, unanchored,
while the whoosh of wind through Los Angeles' streets
cackles and waves her bludgeons of fire.

So often I have seen the smoggy air and fouled water,
plastics floating in every eddy of my body and the body
of the world, just missing my focused attention—
for their shouts of alarm flew away on the white
    sleekness of gulls,
and I felt no caution, running free, insane in the sea
    spray.

* * *

Loud metal clicks and clanks, steam geysers spew
    release,
the powerful, persistent rhythm of gears, thwap
    and slap.
The roar of cars and airplanes, shake and break the air.
The industrial revolution—beginnings of accelerating
    change.

Now the massive global sound ecosystem—
with beeps, alerts, notifications, ads, bells, bits,
    and bytes—
all triggering fight-or-flight responses in our animal
    bodies,
pinging out cortisol and launching our connective tissue
onto rivers of alarm, plastic credit cards in tow!
This culture is incompatible with the continuance

of the living world the way my market basket
cannot hold water.

Climate change cannot be controlled now.
Positive feedback loops are accelerating
beyond immediate regulation; were this a priority
for any country, anywhere. Meanwhile, on my
        mountain,
the rusty tips of infected fir trees wither, while
        bud worms—
now white moths—drift like snowflakes in summer.
Oh sharp edge of shame, fierce foe in this frame.

There are millions of wise ones wielding their weapons
for positive change and restoration—ignored
by the loudest voices cackling out their bad advice.
But the searing truth lands: There is no enlightened
        leadership
at any political helm. The monied elite's weapons
        of war—
obfuscation, fabricated alarms, and denial—
are a war against ourselves and the living world.

※ ※ ※

Still, the complex network of interdependencies—
our living with all beings—makes music in every niche.
Twirling, singing, crawling, punching the sky: I launch
        myself
from the unrelentingly bleak forecasts into action.
I make my soul's sounds. And then the yellow
        spaciousness
of spirit comes prancing in—hahaha, lalala—saying "let
        go"

Up, up, up into the buoyant air! My dejected
   and defeated soul
finds it can breathe again.

When the cup of my time is full,
I hope the only thing left that binds me to the patterns
I have called myself are the unbridled, chiming
sounds of compassion, purpose and courage.

Simple and Hollow

You cannot make my life
smooth and straight
in this rugged landscape.
Suffering may not be optional.
So undress me,
burn my body, and let my dust blow
over the granite cliffs,
blending with pine duff—
little pieces of bone,
food for squirrels and mice.

No, you must make of my life
a woven tangle
like the vining plants
that climb the trellis;
last year's life—
a ready ladder.
Or like the magpie's bundle of twigs,
woven high in the tree branches—
a nest to hold something alive,
pure, and pulsing.

Still, I like the idea of a life
simple and hollow,
like the effortless white bone
of the crane I found by the river.
Make a flute of my bones, why don't you?
My marrow long consumed,
thrown back into the stream—
food for another.

Play me then,
for I have already surrendered
to your rhythms,
finding resistance futile and fraught.
Play me sweetly—
my tempo finally keeping time
with the effortless
and charmed melody
of your tides.

Indeed, the time for change has come.
Let a new form emerge,
and the old cloak of being fall
to the prickly, dry earth.
No longer bone or dust—
but liquid light pooling between
river stones—unburdened, unbound—
a radiance without name.

Circular Pattern

The thermoelectric fan atop
the wood stove—a little drummer,
tapping away at its snare,
'round and 'round,
tacka, tacka, tacka.

Heat sparks the dance
like nature's seamless
cycle of exchange—
the remnants of one life form
leaning into and nourishing another,
an unbroken choreography
of renewal.

Energy and nutrients flow—
producers, consumers, decomposers,
ensuring that nothing
is wasted.

Waste—a trace of existence,
that shapes and is shaped
by the interactions
of countless species.

Life thrives on transformation—
a ceaseless orchestra of giving and taking
that sustains the balance of the world
in every phrase.

What if our economy was built on giving
and taking in equal measure?

What if progress was defined not by consumption,
but by harmony?
What if we designed in a circular pattern—
'round and 'round,
tacka, tacka, tacka.

Warm Water Coral Reefs

1. WHAT IS ON THE SURFACE

We approach the entrance of the trail in the hot,
weighty air that spreads itself like a wool blanket over
the expanse. A small hole in the tangle of roots, vines,
and leaves beckons with greeting.

We enter the humid shade to the boom of surf walloping
the shore. Up and down, we place our feet carefully on
the sharp rock formations, their texture like a petrified
sponge filled with snails, and dangle from tree branches
with their smooth bark and springy arms, making
careful progress toward Survivor Beach. Trees send
seeking roots down for twenty feet in this web mass of
living. My whole body drips easily as the frothy air rises
from the waves below.

Beneath the crashing surf, where sound begins to still,
live the rain forests of the sea: coral reefs, harboring a
quarter of all marine life. Without a habitat, the reefs
and all the life they support will not exist.

2. WHAT IS BENEATH

Corals' quirky trifecta:
Animal, vegetable, and mineral!
She is an animal—a polyp—
with a ring of tendrils surrounding
a central mouth, like her relative
the jellyfish, but upside down
and anchored below.

She partners with plants:
A single-celled algae called zooxanthellae,
which live within her tissues,
feeding her and creating
the flamboyant colors of the reef.

She deposits calcium carbonate, creating
mineral structures—some like plates,
some like trees, some like blankets—
graceful forms, castles on the sea floor
that quell the storms. These guardians of the sea
grow at a rate of just 1 cm per year.

These soft-bodied, tentacled animals,
with their algae guests, glow
purple, blue, green, red—
pigments reflecting light:
A vibrant garden,
a spirited city,
a fluorescent, fragile forest,
adapted to a narrow range
of temperatures and acidity levels.

When water is too warm,
corals will expel the algae
living in their tissues,
causing the coral to turn white—
to bleach.
Like the pale face of my beloved
close to death, the bleached corals
are at risk of dying.

3. WHAT WINDS THROUGH

There is too much going in—
and too much coming out—
of our oceans.

Human activities—
dredging in harbors,
fertilizer-rich nutrient runoff
from agriculture,
over-fishing,
acid rain—
can tip the balance of conditions
conducive to coral life.

With mortality rates high
and growth rates slow,
this living tapestry—treasure
of the world—
may disappear.

It is predicted that this tipping point
will be crossed
in the next ten years.

4. WHAT CONNECTS

The livelihoods of hundreds of millions
of people—and untold millions of marine creatures—
depend on coral reefs,
making them the most valuable system
on Earth for their size.

5. PRECAUTION

News of you, powerful Polyp,
soft as a flower, comes in
millions and billions.
Our lives and yours—
a linked mutuality.

Some people say corals provide
needed services.
Commodifying something so exquisite,
and brimming with enchantment,
degrades the soul. Yet we are all
the sorrier.

Choose whatever convincing
argument you need
to save them.

Walking across Survivor Beach, the surf too wild to
touch, I wonder about traversing again the tangled
territory, back to where the entrance becomes the exit. I
wonder how to dive into the dark—into that place called
civilization—and dismantle its destructive machinery so
that life may continue to exist.

Atoll

Ring-shaped island,
coral necklace rim
like the solar eclipse's
blotted-out middle.
Her ring of fire,
a corona emptying
swirling light seeds
in a spiral.

Aquamarine waters,
salty, sandy shores,
her shape, an embrace.
Her ceaseless tide
withdraws from me,
then floods me again.

Her perfection is there
in my broken marriage—
in my shame that runs
up the stairs
and bites me in the face.
She is shelter from assailing
thoughts more tormenting
than chiggers in the soft
green grasses of Texas!

444 atolls mostly in
the Pacific Ocean,
444, an angel number!

Wading now, where

walking used to be—
Atoll, your nature
lives in me.

The Holocene

The last 11,700 years of time—
a balmy era of human flourishing:
a stable climate enabling the humming rise
   of agriculture,
written history, technological developments,
and exponential urbanization. It marks our transition
from nomadic gatherer-hunters to creators
   of civilizations,
shaping ecosystems—and the planet—
in unprecedented ways.

From millennia of emergence to this pulsing instant,
I stand, untethered to the fields of time,
releasing the burdens of what has been and what may
   come.

I am here—witnessing this dawn, this sunset, this
   moonrise,
and the music of the spheres.
I let go the daily grind of consuming tasks.
I let go of worry for what the world will be in ten years.
I fly far and free beyond my own lifetime,
or the lifetimes of my beloved young ones.

Images from the past and from my remembered
   future—
like living in another land, in a garden by the sea—
waft in and out. Here, buried in snow, I cannot feel my
   hands—
but I feel time itself, layered like frost and thaw.
Each flake a fragment of history, falling endlessly.

In this one composition
I can feel what my whole life has been.

I peer into the timeless.
By that I mean: I take a hike
and run my hands along the granite boulders
pushed up 75 million years ago—
jagged and sharp, like the unusable
histories of wars in this Holocene. But also—
the quartz is crystalline: a crystal ball holding
mysteries I do not comprehend.

I pull out the hand drum
and offer its resonant music—
to time,
to connection and wholeness;
to epochs unknown to me;
to consciousness in this form;
to music—one of the redemptive creations
of our time.

My drum resounds, announcing our place
within vast temporal scales—
I offer myself, my presence as a witness.

Polyculture

Every school is a growing community hub,
    where we solve shared problems together.
Our laboratory garden gets shredded by hail—
    we break, together.
We build cloches for the raised beds;
    we re-make, together.
We share the same sun
    the same out-blown breath.
Our diverse intelligences intertwine—
    Afghanistan, Guatemala, Mexico—
Each perspective nurtured like a polyculture
    of multi-purpose plants in fertile soil.
Each idea stretching toward its purpose—freely.

One small turn of the dial,
    and we are here.

Musings

Most of the days of my life I will not remember.
I will not remember most of my days!
If I had been more skillful,
what would have been the harvests of Wonderful?
Could I have earned a different future—
But oh! To see marigold seeds
become a bundle of black arrows
in their creamy quiver!

Lately, it has been hot, then cold.
Precipitation cannot decide—ice or water?
The ragged edges of autumn swish and swirl,
eddies of indecision.
Scar tissue on my body pulls in or flattens out—
each an ambivalent mending.
But in the dark of night, the Milky Way pours itself
    across the sky,
filling my happy cup.
The valves of my heart's bleating,
open—close—open again.

I wept to see the bobcat blend into the landscape—
his body an invisibility cloak of belonging.
Only his eyes lit up like fireflies.
Meanwhile, my parched garden
and dusty mountain trails keep quiet in their thirst.
My beloved land is not demanding; it has mastered
the surrender experiment.
The trees, already free of leaves,
stand naked—unabashed as I am:
my transparency debt-free.

Table Runner Couture

The coffers emptied,
a lavish expense,
all for the simple grace
of inhabiting my skin—
this texture, that design,
these layers, those underclothes.
The "I will never be cold again" pants.

I sense into the mystery of fabric—
soft stitching, buttons made of shells,
pleasing patterns and rich shades:
tulips and daisies,
pine boughs and leaves.
Dresses comfortable enough
to sleep in—oh! The joy of wearing
pajamas all day long.

These coverings, a delight—
a language, an expression
of feeling, of joy, of whimsy,
of structure, and protection.
But today, I look
like a table runner.

Finally, these fabrics and styles
fail to hold meaning—
appearances unraveling
in light of great loves:
the glistening air in winter,
hovering white mountain peaks
with their wind-blown cowlicks;

the sound of his voice,
the feel of his fur, familiar;
her mind's keenness,
her heart's vulnerability
and awesome strength.
Oh, the delight—
creating sacred spaces,
building soil, growing food.

"Stay," called the table.
Stay still and beautiful.
Just be with the centerpiece of sweet grass,
the purring tabby cat, and the quiet hum
of what matters most:
clean, fertile soil beneath your feet,
the warmth of loved ones in your hands,
the peace of Spirit in the body.
Here, no fabric can hold you.
No threadbare couture—
only this sacred weaving:
earth, love, and breath.

A New Blueness

1.

Work swallowed everything—
the sweet arc of sun,
full moon nights and Orion;
campfires in the desert,
the hollowed-out tree trunk
inviting enchantment—
my youth.

Then wild Iris flower pods
in the field by the river
rattled their music over my heart,
sprinkling seeds of new life
not buried in the past.

2.

Oh grassy meadow,
like a rippled lake frozen,
buffalo berry branch debris—
statuesque against
the white cloud canvas—
I want to be part of you
on this dance floor.

From my window, I see a carnival
of chickadees in the lilac bushes.
I feel the silk scarf of wind flowing
down the mountains' shoulders.
I taste; I savor; I know the delights

of loving you.

3.

I awaken to a draft,
lifting my attention
to the door where winter
creeps in uninvited—where we
deepen our buried bodies
under the bison robe.

This flesh, a worn canvas—
patches fail to mend frayed edges.
I can imagine a day,
at the end of my powers,
the path ahead—unavailable to me.
Just silky surrender.
Time, precious
as an arborvitae's column.

You know about a change in me—
the full circle of return.
So when tracks are lost
in the snowy mountain pasture
that slopes eastward
toward the rocky sun,
may a new blueness,
like a door in the sky,
reveal its secret wonders.

Permafrost

The bluff crumbled into the sea—
    beached like a stranded whale.
Chalk-white and grey strata
    of grass and soil dissolved into swirling waters.
The earth softened;
    her foundations faltered,
and what was once solid,
    transformed.

Transformed pewter rivulets of silt
    snake down fractured cliffs,
sludge cascading around islands of green turf.
    What do these signals convey?
Warmth unlocks a vault of bone, roots and soil—
    entombed for fifteen million years.

Years of carbon stirs,
    unlocked by hands that drill and burn,
its bonds breaking in the friendly air.
    Russet tundra collapses inward,
dotted with ponds that ooze into pools—
    a wound the size of a stadium—
carved into its features.
    What are we seeing here?
We see ourselves—fragile and unprepared,
    in these mirrors of water.

Water once locked in ancient ice
    now joins seas that slowly swell.
Subsea permafrost waits—

a crypt of carbon and methane,
poised to rise.
   Gases climb, steady and unhurried,
breathing into distant cities—
   what the permafrost exhales.
A fragile balance tips.
   And we remember:
nothing stays forever buried.

Buried no longer—releasing all that was contained:
   carpets of cranberries, blueberry bogs,
shrubs and sedges—once firm underfoot—
   now flex into mud and peat.
Life shifts with the land:
   forests drown; tundras bloom;
while murmurs of ancient plagues
   linger in the melt.

We walk on shifting ground—
   vulnerable witnesses to an Earth unraveling,
her primeval secrets murmuring beneath our feet
   in a language we can now hear.

Threshold

Chuk, chuk, chuk, cry the magpies, flying into
   the crystalline chicken yard, stealing cracked corn
   and peas, then perching atop the aspen, the plum,
   and the juniper with her bright blue scales.

Bawk, bawk, bawk, say the contented chickens,
   clucking on their paths of straw.
   Each bowl of seed thrown out—
   a scattering of dreams.

Ma, ma, ma, rumbles Shanta-Ram, the Icelandic sheep.
   This regal king looks right through me
   with his creamy eyes. We carry hay
   into the pasture to the edge of trees.

Crack, pop, clap, groans the ravenous wood cookstove—
   her arthritic doors and levers
   not quite open
   and not quite closed.

Honk, honk, honk, blows the nose as we ride the last
   molecule of moisture in the air
   to its final destination
   in the handkerchief.

Come, come, come, call the vines of ice rounding
   over the trellis—an ice sculpture, a passageway
   to the front door. Each icicle an exclamation mark
   punctuating this exuberant winter.

Sigh, sigh, sigh—I wait at the honey maple desk.
My heart asks to open the gate,
to visit worlds of perception on the other side.
"Come in," calls the brimming field.

Ashes and Seedlings

Susan's ashes came to reside
on the high point of our mountain trail,
with views reaching across the valley
like outstretched arms,
to where the remains of her beloved's body
rest atop Red Mountain.

Morty's ashes were placed
on the round shoulder
of the entryway, by the stone wall,
feeding now a pine tree—
her neon new growth,
a playful presence in the neighborhood.

Liz's ashes were settled in a niche
overlooking the crater garden—
a spruce planted there;
her blueness, a kind
of remembrance.

David Bryan's ashes were laid
at the base of the 400-year-old
Douglas fir we call "Tilting Tree,"
surrounded by a hundred seedlings,
sprouting in the great tree's shade.

Terry's mother and my friend Dee,
the ashes of the huskies
and the cat named Joe,
all came to rest on this mountain—
where doors open to the next adventure,

where we breathe in the possibilities of wild
fragrant seasons.

We ponder death—taste and feel
our transformation in time—
our nakedness, in light
of this inevitability,
raw and awakened.

And out from the shadows flows
a tidal wave of purpose,
a flood of striving toward our most
meaningful lives.

We feel the quiet ache,
or colossal hole left by those no longer here.
We see our destiny in their passing—
a comfort.
We learn from our feelings as guides,
as signposts for the changes we must make—
course corrections.
We gently mend, take in the new landscape of our lives,
and carry on.

Potential

Domino effects in the living systems of the world
are on the move. These ripple effects are severely
harming our planet's life-support systems
and threatening the stability of our societies.

A quiet little aria—part of the most
operatic composition heard by humanity
and the more-than-human world—
has breezed past opening night.

Preventing catastrophe—justly, urgently—
must become the core goal and guiding logic
of a new framework for our lives, while we
find niches of creativity and compassion
in the midst of collapse.

Citizen of the ailing biosphere,
stop the charge forward to grow an economy
that must withdraw its assault on the living world.

I hear. Oh, I grope. I look for the beautiful
questions that will unlock dormant potential.

2.

My throat feels lodged with a pinecone,
these thoughts too jagged to swallow.
Still, I work to digest our predicament,
to settle into a reimagined self—

carried through the small rituals of my days:
the fire, the bread, the loving, the enduring.

I walk—my heavy wet sleeves, sag by the foggy pond.
The mosquito fish splash, and the sweet smell of willow
swirls with greeting.

I stoke the fire—
long sticks jutting, half in, half out
of the popping flames.
Glowing coals welcome the ash cakes
that will become our bread.
I lay the dough upon the embers
and watch as it slowly transforms.
Soon, the spit and clatter of rain
sends us into shelter.

3.

Water falls from the gutter lip,
forming a pool in the decomposing granite—
speaking to me of persistence,
of small moves and the power
of flow.

The little stuffed bison on the bed in the cottage
awaits the delight of my child's embrace:
the heat of her body; the force of her blood;
her daily transformations awakened like thunder.

4.

Citizens: as temperatures soar and glaciers thaw
into to the crash of rising seas—
as extreme weather events demand a place on

front-page news—
you hold the answer in your hands:
Turn from the fire of fossil fuels. Guard the life
    of forests.
Defy the grip of chemical emissions that linger
    without end.

Make small, bold moves
the way water carves a path—to change,
to freedom, to find its balance again.

Potential isn't something given;
it is something discovered in the generous spaces
between intention and imagination.
Look for flow—
where the water wants to go.
Look for the feeling of spark, inside,
waiting for your breath to fan it into flame.
Keep searching.
We are always a becoming.

A Soft Place to Fall

For Brenda

I walk easily up the snow-dusted
mountain slope this dry December—
where sage and Douglas fir grasp hands;
and lay down under the levitating boughs.
How low the sky looks
through the sappy branches.

I summon all my strength
to cross the convincing chasm
of separation,
and wade into the river
of all my kin:
microbes, insects, plants, and animals,
living in silent perfection—
movements synchronized
in complex networks,
balancing nutrients,
managing energy flows:
repairing, regenerating, restoring—
purring ancient rhythms
of interconnection
into being.

* * *

Before, I was seduced
by towering stories—
turn-or-burn snarls of fear-laden doctrines—
manipulations from red-faced greed

with its slick-tongued urgency.
I didn't know another map existed—
though at times,
I heard life's lilt song
penetrating through the noise,
booming now.
I was programmed to work and consume:
feed the machine that fed on me—
uphold and protect the grinding gears of progress.
The living world was a resource—something I
assumed would always be there,
like a bottomless well.
And I reveled in the game:
its comforts, its spoils—
until I saw that neither I, nor any of us,
can survive this bloated way of living.

* * *

Above me, on the rose quartz ridge,
Raven dives on waves of dreams—
her iridescent blue-black wings coaxing
my shadows into the light.
Just off the trail, a dark-eyed junco flutters away,
drawing my gaze from her hidden nest,
holding three pale-blue, spotted eggs,
each the size of a pearl.

The mysteries of what lies ahead—
unforeseen and incalculable—
fold themselves into my arms.
I am inside-out now, belonging to the wild.
I am not afraid—not afraid—of dying;
but gripped and shaken by the fierce pulse of life—

the elegance and splendor that lives in the heart
of the ordinary, while time gallops by
on her billowy mare.

Stillness

Strange, in the midst of coffeehouse music,
to hear the silence speak.
She doesn't debate whether
the climate is changing.
She speaks in the verses of concrete things:
like the yellow blossoms dangling extravagantly
from cherry-colored branches,
vanilla ornaments basking in their own
idea of perfection.

Silence speaks in rhyming light:
the dancing child turning in the sun,
the smiles of friends and their
knowing eyes that wink like lighthouses,
signaling through the haze—Over here!
Here is your cotton-quilted island of comfort,
that pops like corn and pulses
with the rhythms of happy people.

And she spoke to me in the
delicate scent suspended in air—
like a gauzy dress puffed up by the wind,
the sweet fineness of something light:
a feather or silk brushing your skin,
again and again.

Adaptation Plan

Her long shag of strawberry hair
hangs straight in the windless heat,
blue-gray eyes ablaze.
Hands rubbing together
the inner bark of cottonwood
and juniper, with sage brush dust
added to the tinder bundle,
a little cinnamon spice.

A circle of women, like a nest,
will hold the ember she will create—
by rubbing two sticks together
between her tan hands, or by turning
a drill with her bow.

Our ancestors chased fire:
lightning strikes,
forest fires,
lava flows.
They caught embers
and kept them burning—
until someone figured out
how to make a friction fire.

Their primitive technology—
that is not primitive—
shows us how to make fire
with sticks these
800,000 years.

Today, we make fire differently:

great fire balls that killed hundreds
of thousands of people,
dropped from the sky—
an unmasked incinerator.
Splitting atoms,
our great fire wisdom.
What will people say of us
in 800,000 years?

We begin with thanks.
We are at play—
with the bow and drill.
We are relaxed, curious.

The drill flies out.
The bow string breaks!
The burnt depression
on the wood board
needs scraping.

We adjust our approach:
gratitude fueling patience.
We listen for the connection
of two woods.
We put weight into our effort—
the weight of our legs and bottom.

"You don't have to make fire alone,"
she said. "What a ridiculous idea.
Alone is a death sentence.
Take time to prepare everything for ignition;
then go—don't stop. Keep going."

We place the ember in the tinder bundle,

sway it back and forth, flirting with the air.
We blow so gently,
giving the ember room to breathe.
We do not smother
the seed of fire.

An ember. Oxygen. Fuel.
Combustion!
The bundle bursts into flame—
filled with feeling in our hands.

I travel back to the beginning:
Shelter, Fire, Water, Food, Medicine.
I resurrect these ancient relationships—
foundations of community and living.

Thwaites Glacier

In the northern mountains of Montana,
a landscape of breathtaking beauty—
lives Glacier National Park.
Once crowned with 150 majestic ice giants around 1850,
it is now comprised of just a handful of glaciers—
fragile remnants of a vanishing world.
These ancient thrones
are dissolving under warming skies,
their crystalline bodies breaking into fragments
and flowing down the mountainsides.

Once, while backcountry hiking from the park's
    southern border
to Canada, I drank deeply from a melting glacier,
    thinking,
"If you can't drink this water, you can't drink any water!"
A terrible mistake. That night stretched long, as I
dodged a moose and her calf grazing nearby—
the outhouse taunting from far away.
Aiming for a paper cup for a #2 in a tent,
is no small feat. This, I've learned,
is all I know of glaciers.

The Thwaites Glacier, in West Antarctica, is on
    the move.
Broad as the horizon, it spans 80 miles wide,
a frozen expanse rivaling the size of Florida.
It flows steadily into the Amundsen Sea,
losing 50 billion tons of ice each year—
a quiet offering to rising seas.
Alone, it accounts for 4%

of annual global sea-level rise,
its fate intertwined with our own.

Beneath the surface, warm ocean waters
slip through hidden channels,
melting the ice from below,
hastening its retreat—
like a heavy rug slowly sliding off the floor.
As the rug lifts further, it moves with greater ease,
and as the glacier pulls back,
more ice succumbs to the warming tide.

Scientists watch closely, satellites orbiting above,
probes exploring beneath.
The future unfolds through data's revealing lens,
charting climate's complex, intricate trends.

Thwaites holds enough ice
to raise seas by over two feet.
But it serves as a cork for West Antarctica,
its collapse poised to unleash far more.
The Thwaites Glacier tells a story of change,
one it is still writing.

The Ground of Being

I am in the garden—
my ground of being,
where the musky aspen stems,
like white warriors,
flexible and elegant,
pierce the rusts
of autumn.

Tall Valerian stems bow southward,
their white flower umbels sweet, complete.
Fireweed stalks, and their creamy,
feathered headdresses,
flamboyant, cheering,
while Euphorbia march around
the rocky garden beds, confident
in their yellow, green and red resilience.

All the while my inner landscape
rakes and hoes its resentful furrows:
I was betrayed, disappointed.
I was hollow; I was awful; I was blind.
I was naive and ignorant—
a tumultuous being.
I hold my story softly now,
as I would the drying
umbilical cord
of a newborn babe—
my heart tracking
the movement of sun.

This rocky sphere—

lifeforms, elements, global ocean—
booms with sound,
fury, and feeling! Unfolding ahead of us:
a fabric of magnificent forms.
On orbits, like rivers we fly—
through canyons of space.
One trip around the sun:
365 days.

Earth—the size of a nickel
to the sun's front door; the fifth-largest
planet in our solar system; the only
one with liquid water on its surface—
holds space.

185 bioregions I want to know and savor:
mountains, deserts, forests, grasslands, tundra,
savannas of all kinds...
The perfect place for life—
as we have known it.
My heart swells with well-being and awe;
my soul rumbles affirmingly;
my thorny troubles dissolve in Earth's particular
fragrant weight.

Whatever challenges assail you,
take refuge in our protective atmosphere,
slowly moving tectonic plates,
single moon.

And yet—when in hunger, pain, or fear—
how is a protective atmosphere
a part of the equation at all?

In the Earth's quiet turning,
its steadfast rhythms,
we breathe, endure, begin again.
The book of seasons where
all our life's pages are written—
brings structure to chaos and a pulse
to live by.

We are part of something vast
and magnificent!
Some days this can
be enough.

Gleanings

I place before you
the sweet and bitter
harvest of my days—
you, the Giver who delights
in every variation,
every temperament,
every gleaning.

Like the seeking shoots firing up
from the lateral branch underground,
I forge onward,
looking for your light,
and the chance
to blast off in my sugary missile.

Who is to say that sweat-soaked seeking
will not find the abundance
of your favor
at some point in time?

Full On

1 sit in the painted desert sands.
    The green garlands of mesquite,
    creosote, cat's claw and ocotillo
    peddle their medicine in this
    country fair.

The sun is setting.
    The ocotillo on the mountain
    look like hairs on a giant's belly.
    Juniper shade structures—
    little outposts from the heat.

The place hums its music,
    vibrates like the body of bees.
    The silver dragonfly hovers
    by the Rio Grande.

How delicate are these places—
    and the footsteps of my beloved,
    winding their way back to me.
    How precious and hardy he is.
    How joyful and happy he is—
    in this full-on depression.

Oppression

I.

It is the sorrowful news
    that marinates the mind:
    millions of drones grazing
    on fields of soldiers.
    The sorrowful feeling of futility,
    the sorrow of all the life that is being lost,
    the sorrow of human error re-asserting itself
    like a shadow that refuses to stay behind—
    the distant detonators invisible
    but to the stars in the sky
    and their lyric brightness.

Under the awakening constellations,
    I think: some things are not meant
    to live together—
    like the fish and the camel,
    sand in the mouth,
    unfettered economic growth
    and a livable planet.

2.

You exerted insistent pressure
    to mold the idea of our living to your specifications,
    to build the organizational walls
    to your desired height and dimensions,
    your pressured speech, its own cheering section.
    You bullied and ranted and beat your chest like a
        gorilla saying,

"I did that! I did that!"
The gods of your expectations
casting us as actors in a play we never auditioned for.

Yes, yes we said, for there was making up to do—
    making up for the path that didn't quite reach
        the entrance;
    for the manual that didn't have enough pages;
    for the freezing by the campfire.
    Oh yes there was making up to do
    for the "not quite" quality of living.
    And so we sailed on to your coordinates—
    not knowing that your coordinates
    were all you knew of the sea.

3.

No longer a slave of the pattern, of repetition,
    of being the engorged teat ever providing,
    I exchange my innocence for gratitudes galore—
    laughter and levity that sends every oppression
    to its natural death.

Re-configured, I remember my soul force,
    I focus my gaze,
    claw out of the compliance I know.
    For the power of purpose and motivation
    is mine.

Mutualistic Power

If you do not love the living world,
if you do not have a relationship with the living world,
you will not grieve her ill health or death—
until her loss burns your skin.
Grief and love: two knuckles
of the same fist.

Grief is the bone bound
to the bone of love.
There is mutualistic power in these emotions.
Like corals and zooxanthellae:
corals shelter these photosynthetic algae,
who, in turn, provide energy to the coral.
The two live together: two parts
of the same resplendence!

We must carry them both—grief and love—
to see clearly, unvarnished,
and walk forward with open,
discerning eyes.

Immunity

Nature has lost her immunity
to the actions of human beings.

Her fever spikes, her rivers shrink,
her dry skin cracks while oceans swell—
achy with trash, fatigued forests and reefs,
susceptible now to collapse.

What do you see happening
where you are?

Human-caused effects will extend into time—
longer than the entire history
of human civilization thus far,
these hundreds of thousands of years.

From 1900 to the present,
we, the people, are the asteroid impact,
the super volcano, the ice age.
We are the forces changing
the atmosphere.

Not all of us—
just those of us in developed countries
living as we do.

Earthward

When the struggle we thought we had won—
with time and evidence on our side—
stretches out into the distant horizon,
the road narrowing to a pinpoint,
our sight tumbling down the western edge
of this glowing sphere like a waterfall,
lost to all direction or control,
I summon a reverence for life:
stilling the strife within my own mind as I kneel in soil,
planting seeds that may not mature in my lifetime—
the slow work of justice stretching endlessly
    into forever.

Take my hand—let us walk together in the company
of truth-seekers and equality-keepers,
warriors riding the exposed ridges of injustice
    and oppression.
Let us cultivate a reverence for life together:
choosing food that heals the land and ourselves—
foraging, buying local, tending gardens that thrive.
Let us awaken to life on the margins of the machine
    world,
where crickets still sing in the evening.

We can defy every rule or norm that tells us
what we should desire, even as it feels empty and hollow.
We can leave the drunken dance,
enact a reverence for life
that fills every void with loving attention:
noticing, being at play, being present,
and working to eradicate the combustion of fossil fuels.

Let the flashing billboards and neon signs—
remnants of a dying society that lost its way—flicker
    endlessly.
Honor life's sacred thread:
resist petroleum-fed fields with hands that plant seeds
    of renewal—
a quiet rebellion, an act of war.

The first peoples of the Americas endure—
speaking languages shaped by land and stars,
guarding traditions that honor life's web.
Let us join their resistance:
press governments to uplift nations striving
    for balance—
restoration and resilience over greed.

I sit in stillness, cedar smoke spiraling skyward—
listening for the forces that weave life's intelligence.
Here, I align myself and carry reverence like a lantern
into the darkness.

Lungs

He built his home with stone,
wanted to avoid the
use of biological material—
enacting a reverence for trees.

We have planted seeds of change these thirty years,
progress at the pace of one person with a hoe.
Each choice, a chance to rewrite the end—
protect what remains
while the forces of change overwhelm.

The trees fall—
not in the autumn of their life, their decaying
bodies becoming soil for a new generation,
but with the violence of machines:
their roots torn from Earth's core,
their canopies collapsing like lungs deflated.

Each minute, 2,400 more—
a rhythm of loss, relentless, unyielding.
Forests shrink by millions of hectares each year,
a wound the size of nations carved into the planet's skin.

In Brazil, in the Congo, in Bolivia—
the tropics bleed green into barren brown.
Wildfires rage, agriculture sprawls,
and promises to protect, dissolve into bewildered air.

We count the trees as they vanish—
but not the birds displaced,
the rivers cleft,

the carbon unleashed into a warming sky.

Pledges are made—2030 looms—
but saws scream louder than words.

And so we watch, defiant,
as the lungs of Earth gasp for air.
The machinery of avarice—insatiable—
claws its way toward the destruction
of us all.

Cascade

l am the water wheel
　　you empty then fill me ever
　　　　with your weight

l am the ceaseless stones
　　you grind to dust then create
　　　　mountains again

l am the permeable mist
　　you scatter then gather me
　　　　easily

Naked
　　l feel your freshness
　　　　The sweat on you cooling
　　　　　　my skin

Every season is filled
　　with your hot, cool, roaming
　　　　light-filled sighs
　　　　　　Oh sphere, oh orb of my heart,
　　　　　　　　terrain of majesty and wonder!

The days of playing on
　　your ripples
　　　　are long passed
　　　　　　Now just tossed in
　　　　　　　　your waves

l enter the flow without
　　resistance or fear

My nerves alight
    I feel everything as if I
        could die joyously, as if
            no worry or pain is true

My being
    as spacious as
        spirit leaving the body

Your forest liver
    Estuary pancreas
        Soil skin
            Wetlands bladder
                Grasslands hair
                    Reefs heart
                        Apex predators mind

The keystone species
    The symbiont I am
        as a whole
            Every ecosystem
            Every species
            Here.

Hush, Little Baby

Hush, little baby, don't say a word,
Papa's gonna buy you a mocking bird.

And if that mocking bird won't sing,
Papa's gonna buy you a diamond ring.

And if that diamond ring turns brass,
Papa's gonna buy you a looking glass.

And if that looking glass gets broke,
Papa's gonna buy you a billy goat.

And if that billy goat runs away,
Papa's gonna buy you another some day.

* * *

Hush, little baby, close your eyes,
Mama's gonna sing you a lullaby.

And if that song drifts off on a breeze,
We'll listen to the leaves in the Aspen trees.

And if those leaves fall down to the ground,
We'll watch the stars as they twinkle all around.

And if the clouds cover up the sky,
We'll feel the warmth of a hug nearby.

And if the night feels quiet and still,
Know that my love will hold you 'til...

You drift to sleep in peace so deep,
Hush, little baby, it's time to sleep.

Erosional Remnant

We, the people,
comprised of millions of earth-aligned souls,
a mycelial network, immune to extinction—
are resistant rock, distinctive living forms,
able to withstand weathering and denudation.

We understand our social systems
cannot be reformed from the outside—
systems whose intent is grounded
in maximizing profit no matter the cost.

We see and know the capitalist empire is crumbling;
cultural decay around every corner.

We have already transitioned to a new
logic, a new and elegant standard:
If it does not add to life, it does not pass!

Indeed, something has fallen away:
our respect for national leaders,
our support for their monstrous agendas.
Yes, something has fallen away:
the rule of law, the Golden Rule, standards
of truth-telling, integrity, compassion and justice.

But we are truthful.
We do unto others as
we would have them do unto us.
We have integrity.
We are just.
We take care of each other.

And we are busy, weaving webs of interconnection,
building skills to offer our communities, creating
    materials
to design more intelligent and resilient systems—
neighborhoods, towns and cities.
Our networks hum with voices rising.
Our minds are sharp like a mother's attention.
Our hearts are full of creative answers.
Our bodies manifest every bright idea.

We are people with foresight
and are enacting a reverence for all of life—
our kin in the air, on land, and under the sea.
We are putting to use the dung
of hungry power, money power, blind power,
in service of regeneration.
We do not concede, submit or comply.
We serve life; we are life; we are aligned
with the living world.
We know who we are; we know why we are;
we know where we are—
and we are still here.

The media universe does not see us.
But we, the people—an erosional remnant,
are the strongest force on earth.

It is true that something has been lost.
What has been lost is a sleepy
cog-in-the-wheel identity:
an allegiance to a crumbling system
that does not recognize us;
and the mainstream titanic belief that the continuance
of life as we have known it is possible.

But we are building our own social stability.
We are not waiting for the billionaire class
to give us anything, for the best things
in life are already ours. Already ours!

We are not waiting to be granted needed reforms.
We have been forging them with our own hands for
    decades.
We are not pacified by comforts and accumulation,
mollified into a corn syrup-stupor.
We are people of action—focused,
intent on enduring.

A new shape has come into being.
We are present now in this frame—
to protect what remains,
to mend what has been broken,
to restore what has been stolen.

We, the people,
are re-imagining our relationship to life itself:
re-creating our patterns, re-weaving our values and
    habits,
filling our lives with a new level of commitment—
in solidarity with the living world.

Let us stand together, grasping hands—unbroken,
    unintimidated—
inspired by our beauty, our diversity, our resiliency.
We call on all who hear the heartbeat of our world:
join us in shaping lives worthy of this land.

The Voices of Change

*And Collapse says: "This is the first evening I am clear—our
ship has struck the iceberg already. Our upper deck just
hasn't started flooding yet."*

Grandma Rachel holds my right hand
from the world past.
Young Hannah, holds my left hand,
from the world future.
I straddle time,
with somber Spirits.

Sky, Soil and Sea—
lifelines intertwined,
inside us.
Our ecological selves
forming the bedrock
of educational landscapes,
nurturing a new generation
of leaders—
leaders who grasp
our interdependencies,
recognizing the delicate balance
of our interconnected world,
and the vital veins
that sustain it.

*And Hope says: "Tears never stop flowing, but meaning—on
the margins of a vast futility—awakens. The breakdown of
old systems invites new visions to emerge."*

I gather all that we have lost

and lay their soft presences beside me,
in memories' tumble of blankets.

I reach for my displaced kin,
my other skin,
who find solace in our inclusive embrace—
in a place with open doors to learning, healing,
and livelihoods renewed, rooted, assured.
A chance to rebuild, to thrive,
to weave new threads
into the fabric of our shared lives.

Our landlines—equitable economies—take root
in the richness of local soil,
where acts of reciprocity—
nurturing and replenishing the Earth,
and the harmonies of diverse voices blend:
a braided river flowing toward sufficiency.

*And Doubt says: "Will you use me to stop you, or will you
use me to transform?"*

Child in the woman,
Child in the man,
Child in the living spirit—
Be vast as Cassiopeia,
adrift in the bitter cold of space;
small as the tadpole,
drifting in the shimmering light
on the shallow pond.

Be spacious then, child—
find connection, creativity, resilience,
and belonging in this bright day.

And Change says: "I will uproot you. Your roots without soil, will find new capacities you never imagined."

Ceaseless Vibration

Grandmother reverence—
your deeply loving resiliency
in my ceaseless vibration:
constancy, inconstancy—
swimming in the dailiness,
endless—like the litter box's
continual need.
Dust ever drawing down,
settling on everything;
cheatgrass creeping
into every niche of the garden—
all in this skin shell, porous
like woven cloth.

Some days,
I feel unconfined—
moving in the cooing sounds
of your inhaling and exhaling winds.

Other days, I feel bounded,
as fixed as your law of gravity—
immutable.

I have loved you.
But debts tower too high—
choices stretching beyond
your capacity to carry.
What I take is more than you offer.

Our bond, now brittle—
like the desiccated iris pod

filled with black seed,
its stiff stalk teetering side to side.

Body of flesh:
now putrid bloat,
now sinew, now grass.
This unremitting force of change—
our camp, emptying itself
of us.

Grandmother reverence—
I follow the warm sing-song of your humming,
my clenched heart losing its fear.

Light that Persists Unseen

From the corner of my mind,
I hear the airy voices of my ancestors.
Feel their patient footfalls walking
to the rhythm of rampant capitalism
sounding at every turn—
manipulations hammering on the news,
throbbing in the grocery aisle.
It's not a peaceful time,
even for the dead.

But I will look for you
amidst the unraveling.
Work the plow, digging
for the truth of you.
Find you in skinny eyes
that bear hunger's weight.

I will walk your rivers,
climb your bouldered shoulders.
Call to the sheltering clouds
above me.
Find you in my uncertainty
and insignificance.

I will cast my hopeful nets
toward your dry expanse—
Find you in the stability
of having two legs.

Beloved, let me know you
as you were when

we first met,
before the rape was
enacted, before the
destroyer's power became
so absolute.

I will persist like the vibrations
of a plucked guitar string
calling for protective spirits
to come to our aid.

I will make peace in the gap
between what is wanted
and what is real.
I feel a pulse is here.
I am rooted in what was stolen
yet still mine.

Shadow Song

Woman disrupted—
anxiety and rage.
Become present to your
world. Feel what
you are being.

The sad story swirls overhead—
so believable—while underfoot,
the living world goes about its business,
deeply rooted.

Let uncertainty
sharpen your senses—
prying open
your unseeing eyes.

You rail against the new church's
parking lot that paved over the meadow
where you worshiped, yet—
you pave over your pain.

2.

There is a genocide
being inflicted
upon our world
and all our kin.

What will you make of this horror?

How will you labor, love, or endure?
Who will rise from what remains of you?

3.

I embrace you, Grief,
rock you in my arms,
kiss you tenderly,
hum a quiet tune.

I welcome you, Death,
walk down the hallway of memory.
At its end, I cradle your sweet body,
as if your heart still pulsed its divine rhythm.

I hold you, Loss,
carry you forward on my own legs—
into a new land, your corpse a chrysalis,
to re-invent yourself within.

Empathy. Humility. Integrity.
These far-off words linger on my tongue—
their sweet nectar I sip like a tonic
for wounds unseen.

4.

You are there by the broken hoe—
the shards of wood snapped on the rake—
where the sandy soil yields no food.

You are there where the trail
is impassible, dreams implausible;

where the squirrels have not passed by,
baring their woody cones.

You are there in the barren fields—
shades of gray, dusty furrows—
in dread's weight,
its sag and whimper.

You linger in the empty hours—
in the dissonant feeling:
Are we not meant to add to life,
like seeds that germinate so willingly?

Papery Divinity

l look closely at my world—
for its small miracles,
and the perseverance of love:
a common geranium blooming—
coral and cream clusters, papery divinity,
all winter long; pure water and bottomless cups of tea;
the seeking eyes of our black dog—joy,
ready to ignite the neighborhood.
That is who l am.

l can feel it—
the force of cold striking
the rocks. The way a thought
drops in or shoots across my mind's eye,
like a baseball soaring into the outfield—
the swift action that follows: energy,
animation—a kaleidoscope of patterns
moving through air.
That is what l am.

After birth,
this day,
before death—
That is when l am.

The colors are in my eyes—
imagination, story, the labyrinth
of feeling and perception.
Through the lens: a lived journey
in an internal landscape of meaning-making—
That is where l am.

Memory exists like echoes,
resounding in a canyon—
swells and stirrings, vibrating fast or slow,
tight or broad.
That is how I am.

There is a place for what I can hold—
what I can change, offer, celebrate,
conserve, grow, and build—
what I can leave behind for those who follow.
All else lives in another place labeled:
"Genocides, Extinctions, Artificial Intelligence,
National Politics, Aliens."

I am here to live—
and die.
Live in hope;
die in hope.
Work the muscles of restoration;
sound the rhythms of peace—
until the season of an untimely frost.

Deer Botany

I asked him if he knew
all the plants that grow
on Hollowtop Mountain
and her pleated kilt.

"No," he replied,
"Though I'm pretty sure
I've tasted them all."

The deer browse—
their pink tongues
a megaphone announcing
the edible, the medicinal.
No reference books
or YouTube videos,
just their tender tongues telling
and wet noses gleaming.

I read the ingredients list.
The longer the list,
the more apprehension I feel.
It is a language full of fictions,
blaring manipulations—
as if sucrose, high-fructose corn syrup,
barley malt, dextrose, maltose, and rice syrup
are substantially different things!

Do fabricated flavors tell me anything real?

* * *

Here, there is hail that claws the bark
off branches with quick strokes
and confuses the flight of the little gray jay;
ice sheets that slice the cottonwood trees;
cold that breaks all my defenses with one penetrating
  gaze—
and condenses itself
on the transparent glass,
an unwelcome ghostly visitation,
while deer rest under fir tree boughs
waiting for the storm to pass.

I am too old to romanticize or idealize.
Nature will not hesitate to reabsorb me.
But I will not concede to living in a fetid, degraded
  landscape.
"Don't drink that!
Don't eat that!
Don't touch that!"
she says to the children.

* * *

We can feel alone in our exile from the stark real
  world—
alone as a divorce—
but we can also walk outside,
lean into the feeling of the crisp, incandescent world:
where there are no festering hours.
Taste, taste—touch, feel—lick our fingers!
Have a mud and clay massage!

My smoldering hunger roosts in the buffalo berry
  thicket—

with its red fruity flares and stalks of tall winter grass.

Oh to get lost in a gentle land—
walk a well-marked path that flows away from every
    immovable object—
into the summer that awaits: her grassy eyes gleaming.

The Weight of Ice

The world's largest island
at the top of our world,
the Greenland Ice Sheet—
a little hat to Antarctica's boots—
is melting.

Her ancient dome, fractured and flowing,
carves paths to the sea.
Her crevasses, wrinkled like an elephant's skin,
form a vast, patterned plain—
responding to greenhouse gases and warming seas.
Meltwater streams from the surface,
warming her base and accelerating the thaw.
Is her skin of ice collapsing?

How deep do they reach,
these chasms of yielding time?

Once, this reflective ice surface
was a mirror to the sun, a shield of light.
Now, dark earth is seen as the ice fades,
revealing stone and soil long buried.
The land absorbs more solar energy,
further warming the ice sheet,
increasing the melt.
All life on Earth is tangled up
in this acceleration.

If the entire Greenland Ice Sheet disintegrated,
it could raise sea levels by twenty three feet.

What life will grow in this new green land?
What life will vanish?

The numbers speak in centuries, degrees,
gigatons, and millimeters.
The numbers speak of persistent, accelerating decline—
of futures submerged.
But what do the numbers say of us?
Of humanity's place in this unraveling story?

The words of science speak
in a language of their own.
But the weight of ice is not silent.
It cracks and groans—
a language of urgency we struggle to hear.

The weight of ice demands action—
before its cry becomes our own.

Unburdened Heart

To seek forgiveness, unburden your heavy heart,
unveil the story of your conviction; let it
crack, breathe, and dissolve into the still pool
of feeling right.

Allow yourself to imagine feeling light again—whole
     again—
as if the small container of your pain has shattered,
its fragments dissolving into the vast light
     of understanding,
where mysteries replace certainties,
and compassion softens what once felt true.

Freedom grows steadily, unfettered and sweet,
like the black-and-white dog called Shadow,
curled up in the comfy chair—
curious about kisses and hugs,
never having known them before.
He sweeps hearts open like the flying sticks
he catches mid-air, his face dusted with snow.

Let yourself be seen and known,
so kindness may hold you with the utmost care.
Breathe deeply, knowing we are all made
of the same stuff, having but a brief moment
together to share our lives.

Like Shadow's joy in running, his tail held high,
its white tip a flare—what we share
runs deeper and wider than the opinions
     and contentions

that swirl within us, lifeless as ashes.

Embers and Wind

1.

The earth tipped—
and the jolt turned my life upside-down.
All I thought was given—
even seasons—
floated weightless in the air,
as if gravity had
let go.

And there,
in the stems of light
streaming through shattered windows,
I saw sparkling threads in the air,
binding all things—
filaments unraveling, reforming—
like landscapes breaking,
then remaking.

2.

My forest lies still on the ground:
its brittle, gray bones entangled—
a jumble of endings.
Beetles carved their stories in pine bark;
drought wrote the final word.
Now the dry air hums with waiting—
fire holds its breath, poised to enact
its ancient rhythm: balance and renewal
through flame.

3.

The icy river flows eastward,
just beyond the garden gate—
carrying my resistance.
Above me, the pterodactyl fliers
cry their blue music.

I turn the soft, sweet soil—musky with scent—
the soil of creation, preservation, and destruction,
composting all my days into fertile ground.

Over my shoulder lies an intact web of life;
ahead stretches collapse.
I offer myself to this moment:
my breath to the wind, my hands to the earth—
barefoot on this valley road I cannot yet make peaceful.

Calm

I feel a calm before storms,
 Tumult that will touch my living.

I hear there is a wobble
 In the Earth's rotation.
 So much water is
 Pumped out of the ground,
 The Earth's axis is shifting.
 Such is our impact
 As a species.

I learned she planted a garden
 Before she knew how,
 But the Giver knew.
 Seeds sprouted to life
 In the rich soil and light.
 She did not know how
 This miracle came to be;
 She just knew enough to plant
 The seed.

I see he lives from the waste stream,
 So brimming it is, he limits harm.
 His children deride him,
 But he is immune to their scorn.
 He wants to be a change
 So they might inherit
 A livable planet.

I look around for clues,
 I listen for what remains silent

In my weaving with life.
I dig for the recipe that blends
Energy and heat—
The alchemy that makes
Courage rise.

Listen

My six year old has suffered five fractures this year,
her bones filled with lead.
My daughter, thriving on organic food,
hiking 10,000 foot peaks, has osteopenia.
The lead poisoning came in employee housing,
Yellowstone National Park.

My three-year-old scoots down the stairs,
pauses, then declares with glee:
"I have something to say...I like cake,"
his red hair and incandescent innocence gleaming.

My new baby, walking and curious,
demands constant vigilance.
Every moment now centers on
keeping everyone alive.

The Atlantic Meridional Overturning Circulation
    (AMOC);
The mass death of coral reefs;
Greenland's melting ice sheets;
The collapse of West Antarctic Ice Sheets;
thawing permafrost; deforestation—
You ask me to understand, act, and give time
to this predicament we all share?

2.

The collapse of global tipping points

will still the heartbeat of Earth's climate.
The effects on our shared home—
incalculable, far-reaching, irreversible.

Listen: The relentless exploitation of ecosystems
on a finite planet will always meet hard limits.
When those limits are crossed, Earth's systems falter.
And we are so many now. Urgent action
is needed to protect the fragile life-support systems
that sustain us all.

3.

It is time to fly into the expanse, never alone,
carried on the wings of snow geese flying
above Freezout Lake, Montana—
30,000 strong, lifting off in unison,
twisting and turning as one before settling again.
A crystal in their pineal gland guides them,
keeping them in the right spot.

Our arm-like wings and beautiful minds
are attuned to coordinated flight.
We, too, can find our right spot
in this turbulent season of change.

4.

I choose the paper cup over
polystyrene that will never decompose
while corporate entities pollute
on a massive scale, unchecked.
I nourish my children with food free
from fossil fuel's stain, while industrial

agriculture depletes soil,
pollutes water and air, razes forests.
I stay present—eyes fixed on the baby,
my heart beating in rhythm
with the Earth's grand current, the AMOC.

Oh, generous Giver, you animate
my fleeting life and the habit of my grief.
Oh, endless tears that fill a trench,
your shadows cannot drown
the flame of my small candle.

Call and Response

Rocks on rugged paths
pummeled my feet
on all sides,
as I traveled
in broad sweeps
across this crusted orb.
The days carved themselves
into my glances,
the weight of cargo
wearing out my joints—
energy under this big sky.

Roiling curiosity
and incredulity,
I watched the machinery of my life—
geared toward repetition,
my part rehearsed
over and over,
nose to the assembly line—
quest for certainty
and significance.

Beloved, you have traveled
through challenge-filled years,
worked your way around
every obstacle
on the cycles of day
and night.
Your determination flashes

underneath your lashes—
strength under this big sky.

Churning habit of will,
tsunami of tenacity,
chariot driver, entrepreneur—
your eyes on every flower—
quest for connection,
and variety.

2.

My face fell
when I saw you
laboring over your book.
We try to put out
a blazing fire
with brooms dipped
in pails of water.

I come to stillness now,
in your purring,
exhausted—
for we have lost
even the promise of summer.

I dig in the garden,
hands growing numb
with the effort.
The blossoming pear trees—
a chorus of cheering.
Hops, flamboyant
in their neon green cloaks,
unselfconscious,

roots running beyond my sight.
In you lives my connection
to wonder, joy and sanity.

You dig the trench
for the drainage pipe,
mend the fences, coax the sheep
with your bucket of oats.
Your hands—rough as gravel—
on my body.

3.

I stand at the edge
of the Tobacco Root Mountains,
where water flows through the town—
to sense the power and range
of the tumbling river,
to feel the winds swirling up and down
the mountain's skirts—
these thousands of years.

I walk in the foothills
and taste the eternal gooseberry,
chokecherry, and rose hips
growing on the old dump.

Prairie Smoke

Dust tracked my wandering path
    through hot, arid fields:
    the muddy muck of river trails
    and cow pastures,
    sheer mountain passes,
    desperately hot valleys,
    through thorny griefs and confusion,
    with tender feet and frail tales.

Open spaces explored inside—
    fleshy wounds and stiff scars,
    laden smells and tousled hair.
    A home in life's interchange,
    a home in life's unfolding, awakening, tenacity,
    a home in life's grit and grace.

That is where I found you—
    in abandon,
    where the flooding water
    takes off her boots—oh bride of revival!
    And in the heat of the day,
    the pink Prairie Smoke flower
    buds, blooms, and explodes.

All the Darknesses We Have Lived

A gnawing interrupts my sleep—
like a bushy-tailed wood rat
amassing her herbs.

Do you feel it—
a desperate need
to climb out of the
industrial river?
To find lungs to breathe
clean air in a new land,
wings to achieve flight,
legs to walk
where fins once were?

To be other than a cog
in the war machine—
complicity
extinguishing citizens of the
vibrating world?

The newborn sheep
all legs and lashes—
his whole body a trembling awakening
cries, while a canyon of sorrows
sings of infinity and my
distant purity.

Are we not beings of vast potential?
Is this the best we can do?
Must we be monotonal
in the presence of imposing sound?

Must we be an enemy
to life itself?

That day when the final tally was given,
I found a ram lamb—
whose broken horn had bled
tar-like down the right
side of his face, his yellow eye
barely visible, while the neighbors'
voices sang like a blackbird
in boisterous celebration.
There was a putrid smell.

Yet stars will watch our plight, saying:
"ooooh and ahhhh," their twinkling cringing.

And when morning dawns,
the last star we can see will strike down
all the darknesses we have lived.